Test your

Personal Skills

GENE CROZIER
AND GARETH LEWIS

Series editors: GARETH LEWIS & GENE CROZIER

Hodder & Stoughton

A MEMBER OF THE HODDER HEADLINE GROUP

Orders: please contact Bookpoint Ltd, 130 Milton Park, Abingdon, Oxon OX14 4SB.
Telephone: (44) 01235 400414, Fax: (44) 01235 400454. Lines are open from 9.00 – 6.00, Monday to Saturday, with a 24 hour message answering service.
Email address: orders@bookpoint.co.uk

British Library Cataloguing in Publication Data
A catalogue record for this title is available from The British Library

ISBN 0 340 802405

First published	2001
Impression number	10 9 8 7 6 5 4 3 2 1
Year	2004 2003 2002 2001

Typeset by Fakenham Photosetting Limited, Fakenham, Norfolk.
Printed in Great Britain for Hodder & Stoughton Education, a division of Hodder Headline Plc, 338 Euston Road, London NW1 3BH by Cox & Wyman Ltd, Reading, Berkshire.

im the Institute of Management

The Institute of Management (IM) is the leading organisation for professional management. Its purpose is to promote the art and science of management in every sector and at every level, through research, education, training and development, and representation of members' views on management issues.

This series is commissioned by IM Enterprises Limited, a subsidiary of the Institute of Management, providing commercial services.

Management House,
Cottingham Road,
Corby,
Northants NN17 1TT
Tel: 01536 204222;
Fax: 01536 201651
Website: http://www.inst-mgt.org.uk

Registered in England no 3834492
Registered office: 2 Savoy Court, Strand,
London WC2R 0EZ

Contents

Introduction

The *Test Yourself* series covers a wide range of skills, competencies, capabilities and styles that all contribute to our uniqueness as individuals and our performance in the workplace. Some of these qualities can be measured directly by objective tests that we call psychometric tests, but others are rather more complex and need to be assessed or evaluated using a range of other methods. Our impact on the workplace, and in particular our ability to achieve business results, is influenced by a complex pattern of behaviours, values and attitudes – the combination of which is described as personal effectiveness. Increasingly, organisations are looking for people whose repertoire of personal skills allows them to maximise their impact within and outside the organisation.

This book is one of a pair of books and deals with the personal skills that contribute to our success. The other book, *Test Your Business Skills*, deals with the practical aspects of our business flair. These books represent the two complementary facets of our personality that contribute greatly to our success in life.

The chapters in this book follow this sequence:

- Chapter 1: The impact of personal skills – the background to the subject
- Chapters 2 to 6: Test your personal skills – an opportunity to assess yourself against a detailed inventory of personal skills, divided into five families

- Chapter 7: More issues that affect personal success
- Chapter 8: Putting it all together – how to improve your skills

By the end of the book, you should have gained a detailed insight into the key skills that contribute to your success and have identified some action points for the future.

The impact of personal skills

Introduction

The search for the ingredients of personal and organisational success is probably as old as history. Certainly the qualities of successful leaders have preoccupied many great writers from Greek and Roman times. The sheer diversity and success of books with titles like *How to be Successful in . . ., Awaken the Giant Within, How to Become Your Own Boss* and so on, prove the importance this subject holds for all of us. Very few people do not want to achieve success in some form, yet the formula that we can use to maximise success is not so easy to find. Even when we read the autobiography of somebody famous, it is very rare that we can take away a clear action point that will transform our lives.

In management terms, the models we use to identify and to develop leaders have undergone considerable evolution over the last 150 years, so much so that managers are now confronted with an increasingly diverse toolkit of philosophies, frameworks and tools to develop themselves and their employees. This diversity comes from the fact that there are radically different approaches towards the achievement of business success, each of which has its own merits and limitations.

The birth of personality theory
In the last century, the seeds of modern personality theory in psychology were sown with the work of Galton. Galton examined the adjectives we associate with leadership and from this huge lexicon of words started to cluster qualities

under some main headings. This work was to form the foundation of work by psychologists on the personality factors that influence an individual's behaviour.

Personality theory has now generated a considerable body of knowledge and tools in the form of psychometric instruments. These are used increasingly by organisations to select and recruit their employees, based on one simple fact: job performance can be predicted by an accurate assessment of personality and aptitude.

The age of scientific management

The twentieth century also saw the birth of modern scientific management, based on the notion that effective management lay in the knowledge of special management techniques. This approach was supported by the emergence of mass production techniques and in the importance of logistics during the two World Wars. The idea that successful management was all about theory and the application of special techniques led to the creation of a professional and an educational approach towards developing managers that is still reflected in the content of many management courses.

The competence-based movement

Modern trends towards increased competitiveness and globalisation have forced many organisations to explore alternative approaches. In the UK, for example, the competence-based movement has revolutionised the whole approach towards management development, leading to the development of a whole series of new programmes that rival the traditional MBA, but also encouraging the transformation of many traditional programmes into a more practical approach. The movement grew out of a feeling that the way we developed our managers was too theoretical and can be summed up by the phrase, 'It's not what you know. It's what you achieve that is important'.

Competence-based programmes, therefore, place a lot of emphasis on the demonstrable, practical skills of managers, which are developed in the workplace.

A new approach

Yet even this practical approach does not provide all the answers. Faced with an increasingly complex and chaotic world, many companies are finding that the logical, functional approach to achieving results does not solve their problems or even necessarily improve performance. Today, we see an increasing number of successful companies turning away from this functional approach to a more inspired approach to identifying the recipe for individual and organisational success.

Here are several examples:

For a successful financial company based in America, the UK and Australia, with many offices worldwide, the impact of several mergers taught them that, in their own words, it is 'the chemistry of the team' that matters the most. They talk about a focus on the feeling within the organisation – a sense of excitement, of appreciation of each other's qualities, of making the company a fun place to work in. They instinctively know whether the fit between team members is right and have the openness to deal with issues when they arise. When they talk of recruitment, they do not list the financial acumen of individuals or describe a typical personal profile for employees. Instead, they talk of a 'good citizen', someone who is confident in their own abilities but who is widely read and with a range of skills they can bring to the table. They rarely recruit people through traditional means; instead, they 'court' potential employees through their networks.

This approach also recognises the fact that individual success is also defined by and dependent on team culture.

The same approach is adopted by a technology company, which used previously to seek out professionally renowned individuals with good negotiating skills. Now, they only see the technical skills as being the entry card. What they are looking for are unusual individuals with the ability to think outside the box and, most importantly, to be able to see that the best technical solutions are not necessarily the best business or management solutions in the long term.

New approaches to management

It is obvious that there has been a significant shift in recent years away from the scientific approach to management towards a more sophisticated human relations approach. We have developed a deeper understanding of the fact that the motivation of workers is a key factor in their productivity at work. Organisations now have to work much harder to retain skilled staff and we now take it for granted that investment in people is as important as investment in other aspects of business or organisational life.

Organisational priorities are changing. This is the information age and the knowledge economy. We will surely see an acceleration of the growing importance of the skills, capabilities and knowledge that people hold and for many organisations it will be their most important or their only asset. Protecting intellectual capital in the form of acquired knowledge and people can only be achieved if you know what you have.

All of this explains the increased attention being paid by organisations to the potential contribution individuals can make through a better understanding of their personal skills repertoire, not just a matching of personality to the nature of the business.

Increasingly, we see a greater dialogue between employers and employees in their joint search for success. Social contracts between the two are becoming increasingly sophisticated as organisations seek to combine strategic direction with performance management, employee incentive and reward schemes, training and development – all within a single integrated framework. Individuals are increasingly able to place their personal aspirations and agendas high on the list of issues when talking to their employers.

The issues involved are complex and people need a common language and models to move forward. This explains why the competency movement has found such favour in many organisations. Organisations are increasingly using the notion of competence as a language to describe the skills that underwrite their organisational development. The particular blend of skills, knowledge, qualities and attitudes that go towards excellent performance at work are often explicitly called competencies, but are also referred to as personal effectiveness. Some of the most sought-after personal skills include:

- teamworking skills
- leadership qualities
- interpersonal skills
- customer relationship skills
- self-awareness and self-development.

A unified model

One very simple way of reconciling these different approaches is to view your actions as a process model. The **inputs** are who you are as a person, ie your **personal skills**, which in addition to in-built personal abilities, include your experience and expertise. You then apply these skills to the job in hand (**the processes**) and your ability to apply these effectively in a business context can be referred to as **business skills**, in other words, a set of **behaviours**. Finally, your success in this area can be measured by hard, quantifiable **outputs** that are **functional skills** or **competences**.

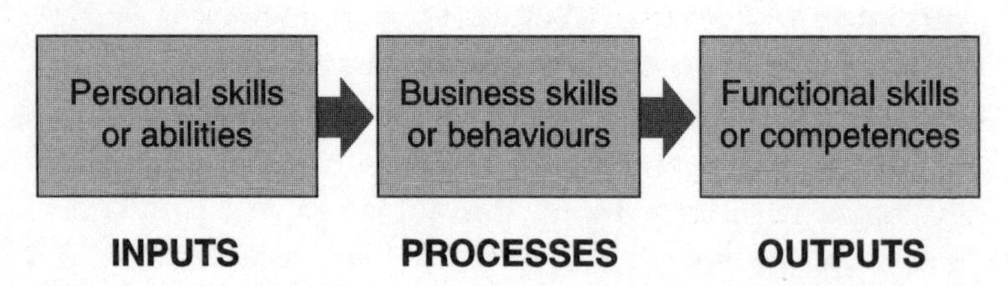

As an example, let us take one important responsibility of a manager, that of *developing teams effectively*. It is obvious that this simple statement covers a wide range of skills, which can be divided into the following three areas.

Personal skills

Some of the personal skills that might make someone a great team-builder include:

- **empowering** – provides inspiration and motivates others
- **results driven** – wants to achieve results
- **development orientation –** believes in developing others, a natural teacher or coach

These skills are a complex mixture of things – values, attitudes, personality factors, knowledge and experience. They are a melting pot of personal characteristics that define our preferences and capabilities. Most importantly, they represent skills that can be applied to almost any situation. The range of skills and qualities involved here obviously form the content of this book.

Business skills

In every work situation, we can then turn these personal skills into a repertoire of roles, behaviours and actions that will have **impact** on the organisation and people around us. Our ability to transform our personal potential into business results represents our business skills. For team development, these might include:

- managing change
- negotiating skills

- evaluating and improving business performance
- team-building skills.

The range of business skills that seem to be in demand from modern organisations are the subject of the sister text *Test Your Business Skills* in this series. The different role models and management styles involved are also covered in *Test Your Leadership Skills* and *Test Your Management Style.*

Functional skills

Finally, our impact in a business environment can be measured through our ability to perform key tasks or achieve outcomes to a clearly defined standard of work. Many of these tasks will be more functional or technical in nature. In many ways, these types of skills (competences) are much easier to identify, because you can usually quantify some clear end product. For team development, these might include:

- carrying out effective appraisals
- creating effective development plans
- planning development plans and generating effective proposals to gain support
- coaching, counselling and mentoring skills
- training, running workshops etc.

The MCI Standards for Managers that form the base of many qualifications in management in the UK have been covered in the title *Test Your Management Skills* in this series. There will also be a range of self-assessment aids in the series, dealing with specific functional areas, such as Finance or IT.

Of course, in real life, we behave in a unified way and there is real overlap between these three approaches. However, this input–output model does match reality in that our business success is affected by the following:

- All three areas are closely interlinked and any weakness in one area will affect our total success.
- The ultimate source of our practical abilities lies in our repertoire of personal skills, which, while they may allow us to do almost anything, may be difficult to link directly to our achievements in the workplace.
- Many people tend to focus on visible outcomes rather than the underlying success factors.

We hope this guide will encourage you to consider ways of developing your personal skills in the future.

Summary

In this chapter, we have claimed that the approach towards management development has followed the evolution of personality theory and industrial change. The main approaches towards measuring potential and success reflect an emphasis on:

- **the personal skills** or *competencies* of individuals that represent their potential to achieve results, based on complex personality factors, experience and expertise;
- **the roles and business skills** people demonstrate within the total context of their working environment; and

- **the functional skills** or *competences* that demonstrate an individual's ability to perform something in the workplace to a defined standard.

Each approach has its own advantages and disadvantages, but there is clear evidence that organisations are placing greater emphasis on the personal skills of employees.

Over the next five chapters, we will provide you with an opportunity to review your own personal skills in detail.

Testing your Personal Skills

Introduction

We have divided these personal skills into five families:

1. Managing self
2. Communication
3. Relationships
4. Thinking skills
5. Getting things done

Each family represents a collection of individual skills or competencies that fall into a natural grouping. Each chapter covers one family, which is structured in the following way:

- **A family overview,** providing a general description, a map of the competencies involved.
- **Individual competency definitions** for each of the competencies, containing an overview and examples of key indicators to help you judge your relative performance in each one.
- **The assessment section**, allowing you to evaluate your performance in the family.
- **Developing skills**, a section that provides specific advice on how to develop your skills in the family.

Family 1: Managing self

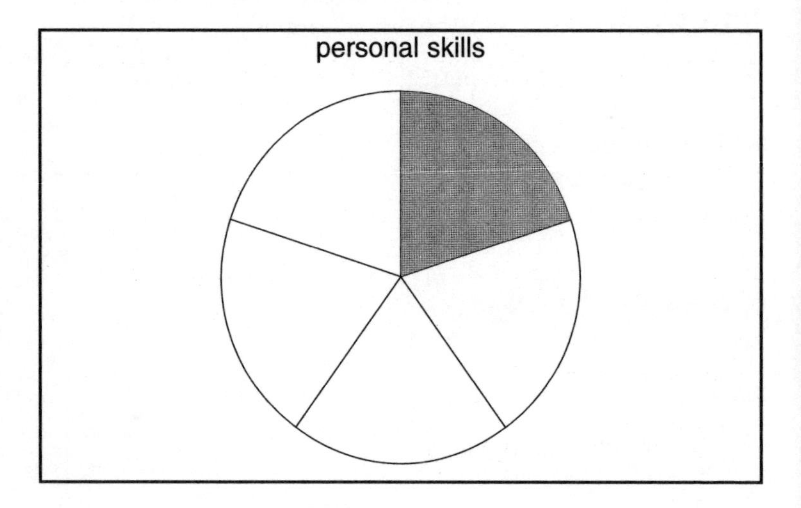

While the other families of competencies deal primarily with the way that we approach the world around us, this family is concerned with the way that we organise the inner world of our own realities. We develop habits, behaviours and approaches to the external world, as a result of our own individual inner world.

Some of our preferences are intrinsic, in that they precede experience – we carry them into the situations and circumstances we face in life. Some are extrinsic, in that they represent our responses to what happens around us. But it is this whole repertoire of behaviours and skills, which we use to react to the world around us, to tackle situations, to cope with circumstances and to grow and develop, which are relevant in this family.

These responses and behaviours get organised into patterns or habits that we use to cope in the world. In a working environment, we need certain aspects of motivation, discipline and resilience in order to thrive, as we do in any social and co-operative situation. The ways that we tackle such challenges – our style and approach – differ from one person to another. So does our ability to gain enjoyment and satisfaction from the things that we do.

This family of competencies looks like this:

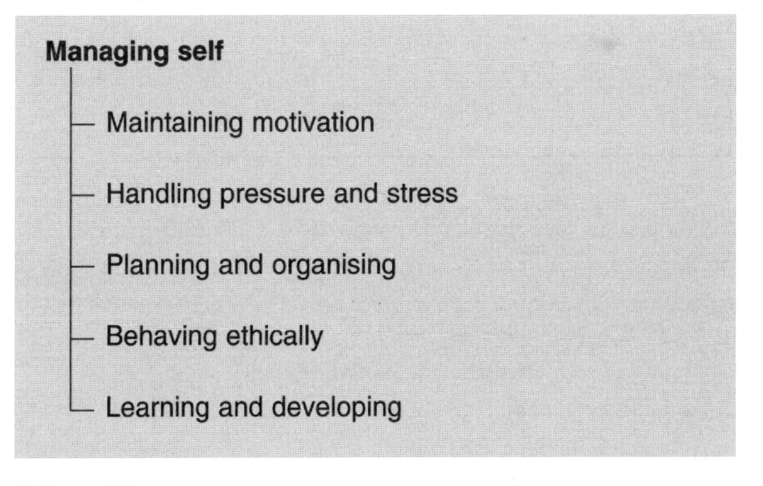

Role model

As with all of the families, we shall ask you to think of people you know who might exemplify these competencies. Before you examine each aspect of the family in more detail, try to take a more holistic view. Look at the map and try to think of people in your family or social life, in your work experience or in the public domain who you would judge to be excellent 'self-managers'.

- What is it they have or that they do that is different from other people?
- What helps them to be so good at managing themselves?
- How much of this can I copy?

Maintaining motivation

Overview

This competency is to do with how we manage our appetite for life and how we keep ourselves motivated. Notice that there are a lot of words and terms with a positive bias. This is no accident. We talk about a positive outlook, optimism, enjoyment and satisfaction. These are litmus test terms for this area.

Positive indicators

Good motivation is:

- being positive in outlook
- being keen to take on challenges
- being go-getting
- having drive
- taking initiative
- showing enjoyment
- gaining satisfaction from activities
- taking control
- being able to work towards goals
- having confidence in self
- having determination to overcome obstacles
- being energetic and enthusiastic
- celebrating success.

Negative indicators
Poor motivation is:

- being sullen
- being pessimistic
- lacking control
- having a 'victim' mentality
- lacking self-confidence
- lacking energy.

Illustration

One of my colleagues asked me, 'If you were independently wealthy, what would you do with your wealth?' I said I'd invest in young companies to help them get off the ground. It was at that point I realised if I would do this as a vocation, why didn't I do it professionally? In a way, Amadeus is my fantasy company because I was so determined to get into the industry and create a venture capital firm. [I got the impetus to succeed when] my parents encouraged me to believe I could do anything I wanted to do if I applied myself. It doesn't come without hard work. It's a formula; it's not luck.

Anne Glover, Managing Director,
Amadeus Capital Partners

Handling pressure and stress

Overview
For most of us, life is very rarely simple. We have to deal with pressure from the world around us. This pressure can

come from many sources. These include life events such as relationships, birth, death and illness, maintaining home and lifestyle, as well as generally just coping in a complex world. And all of this before we even get to work, with all of the stress that that involves.

Illustration

In 1999, the Institute of Management and UMIST surveyed 5000 managers for their Quality of Working Life report. Among the findings were:

10% worked more than 61 hours a week
33% worked more than 51 hours a week
71% said work was having a detrimental effect on their health
79% said work was damaging their relationships with spouse or partner
68% also said that long hours reduced their productivity.

This illustrates all too clearly why we need to develop skills to help us cope with all of the things that life and work throw at us.

Positive indicators
Good copers:

- are confident in difficult situations
- are determined
- have stamina and resilience

- manage their own emotions
- cope in a crisis
- pay attention to their own health and well-being
- are able to relax
- have balance in work and life.

Negative indicators :
Bad copers:

- are moody
- are prone to 'blow up' in a crisis
- are depressed or have a negative outlook
- are constantly worn out or tired
- let their work and relationships suffer.

Planning and organising

Overview

Planning and organising are about being able to order our lives and being able to use our time and activity effectively. In general, it is about being 'on top of things', rather than being submerged in the ebb and flow of the demands of everyday life.

It involves a number of aspects. Firstly, our activities tend to be directed. That is, we are able to look to the future in terms of what we want to be doing and what we want to be achieving. This is in contrast to just 'taking life as it comes'. Then, we are able to make choices in relation to our actions and efforts. We can prioritise and we can make decisions about what is important, compared to those things that are less important or less relevant. Finally, we are able to plan our lives and our activities so that we work towards positive outcomes in an efficient manner and organise the resources needed to do this.

Positive indicators
Good planners:

- are future-oriented
- set and work to objectives
- are in control of events
- are pro-active
- work to schedules
- are organised
- are aware of priorities
- act and work efficiently.

Negative indicators
Bad planners:

- are not on top of work and life activities
- are reactive
- are always fighting fires
- have disorganised working space.

Behaving ethically

Overview
In times gone by, not only was it easier to behave ethically, it was difficult not to do so. The values of the church, the state, society in general and organisations within it were built into the fabric of our relationships with others.

More recently, the rules that went along with these influences have loosened off. In a complex world, with substantially greater freedoms, we have to make many more choices for ourselves.

Paradoxically, whereas organisations traditionally employed us primarily as units of production, they now seek to engage us as fully functioning social and ethical beings. The human relations school of management has triumphed and there is an appropriate focus in organisations on social behaviour, motivations, the 'psychological contract' and so on.

In organisations, then, we are judged as individuals by our behaviour and by the decisions we make. In such environments the integrity of our behaviour becomes an important issue. It leads to such considerations as:

- Does he/she do what they say they will do?
- Do they treat people with fairness and reasonableness?
- Do they act with integrity?

On the other side of the coin, behaviours such as lying, cheating customers or colleagues, manipulating, abusing or bullying staff are, quite rightly, disapproved of.

On the organisational front, we have seen the need to protect people who bring to light unethical behaviour by individuals or organisations – the so-called 'whistleblower's charter'.

Positive indicators
Behaving ethically involves:

- telling the truth
- doing what you say you will do
- challenging inappropriate or unethical behaviour
- treating all people with respect.

Negative indicators
Not behaving ethically involves:

- treating people poorly
- saying one thing and doing another
- breaking the rules of conduct and behaviour
- taking pleasure in the plight of others
- manipulating others.

Illustration

So many people would say to me, 'Larry, you've got a wife and three children, you can't afford these principles.'

Just recently, my son said to me, 'Daddy, I don't think I've ever told you this before, but I was very proud of the stand you took in those blacklisting days.' Well, you can't buy that.

Larry Adler, harmonica player, on his refusal to 'name names' to the McCarthy Un-American Activities Committee

Learning and developing

Overview

Learning and developing are perfectly natural for people in any circumstances as they go through life. However, there are a whole range of reasons why people in normal social and working situations need to be open and skilled in developing their own capabilities.

Firstly, we change as people. As we mature, grow older and live through more of life's experiences, we respond to these by learning and adapting our behaviour and developing our capacities to respond to different situations and to respond to them in better ways.

The need to do this is in the world of work is compounded by the rate at which organisations are changing and as the requirements on us are changing alongside this. With the advent of the revolution brought about by the Internet and new technology and the resulting new business models and ever more competitive environment, we are required as adults and citizens to learn new skills to keep up. In the working environment, we also require more than just skills to master the new technology and newer ways of working. In management, for instance, we are understanding the need to develop a wider repertoire of skills – over and above the technical/professional skills that were traditionally required. We also need to be leaders, to have good communications skills and to develop good 'people' skills – in fact, all of the skills that are referenced in this title, and the companion title *Test Your Business Skills*.

In addition, the balance of responsibility for our development has increasingly shifted from the organisation to ourselves. It is important that we take responsibility for our own development and learning. Developing yourself is a set of skills in its own right.

Positive indicators
Skilled self developers:

- set high but achievable goals
- assess their own strengths and weaknesses
- plan their own development
- seek out challenges and new experiences
- learn from experience
- have a track record of developing new skills
- take on new responsibilities
- are open to new experiences
- adapt to changes
- seek feedback on own performance.

Negative indicators
Bad self developers:

- don't seek or reject feedback
- get 'stuck' in positions or jobs
- have a poor understanding of own abilities – particularly weaknesses.

Assessing your self-management skills

?

Test Yourself

Now it is time to assess yourself. For each competency, consider the highs and lows and then rate yourself on a scale of 1 to 5, with 1 being poor and 5 being a role model. Then ask a colleague to rate you as well. Take your own scores and add them together; then divide by the number of competencies (in this chapter there are five) to get your average score for this whole family. Do the same with the third party's scores. You will end up with two numbers between 1 and 5, which indicate where on the scale you rate yourself and where somebody else rates your performance in this family as a whole

Maintaining motivation

Low: Lacking in self-confidence. Can be seen as negative and de-motivated. Not easily influenced by the energy and enthusiasm of others.

High: Self-motivated, with a natural optimistic and 'can-do' streak. Able to sustain motivation through difficult times. Able to energise and enthuse others.

Role model	expert	competent	inconsistent	poor
5	4	3	2	1

self-assessment ☐ third-party assessment ☐

Handling pressure and stress

Low: Negative mental attitude and lack of enthusiasm. Don't manage their own emotions: moody. Show physical signs of distress. Poor and shoddy work. Illness and absence.

High: Cope even in difficult circumstances. Show energy and positive attitude. Relaxed and energetic in appropriate circumstances. Good balance between work and life outside work.

Role model	expert	competent	inconsistent	poor
5	4	3	2	1

self-assessment ☐ third-party assessment ☐

Planning and organising

Low: Always one step behind the game. Act in a rush and a panic. Not in control of their own working activities and timetable. Late in delivering or don't complete tasks at all.

High: Highly organised and in control of their own timetable. Work in a planned and orderly fashion. Deliver results on time. Have a systematic approach to organising work and activities. Efforts focused on priorities.

Role model expert competent inconsistent poor

5 4 3 2 1

self-assessment ☐ third-party assessment ☐

Behaving ethically

Low: Have not earned or have abused the trust of others. Discrepancy between their words and their behaviour. Have crossed a line in terms of what is accepted to be reasonable behaviour.

High: Known to have integrity. Widely trusted by colleagues and those who know them. Likely to have taken a stand against people or organisations who have transgressed.

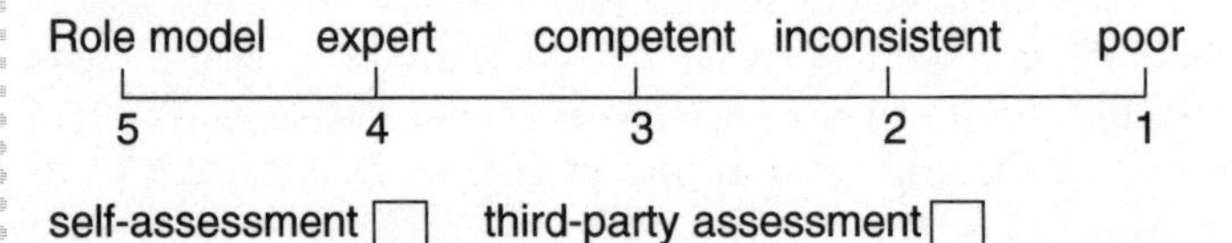

self-assessment ☐ third-party assessment ☐

Learning and developing

Low: Have a poor record of developing new skills. Don't seek out challenges. Don't learn from experience. Have few or no plans for own development.

High: Evaluate and know own strengths and weaknesses. Have practical and up-to-date plans for development activities. Take on challenges.

Role model	expert	competent	inconsistent	poor
5	4	3	2	1

self-assessment ☐ third-party assessment ☐

Average score for self-management:

self-assessment ☐ third-party assessment ☐

Developing self-management skills

The first stage of developing in any of the families of skills in this book is to know and understand where you are. You should now have this picture from the previous pages. It is particularly important to pay attention to the third-party assessment.

If this corresponds to your own self-assessment, then at least you have some confirmation of what your strengths and weaknesses are. You can acknowledge and feel proud of your strengths, and then turn your attention to the weaknesses.

However, if your assessments don't correspond, then this begs questions about the accuracy of your self-knowledge. Check on the objectivity of this third-party assessment and try to verify it by seeking other opinions. This kind of feedback can sometimes be a shock. What you should try to do is to seek accurate information as to what lies behind those assessments, without trying to deny them. What do other people see as your behaviour, that you don't see so well yourself?

This should provide the basis of powerful remedial action. In addition to this, here are some other things you might explore:

- Do a motivation health-check for yourself.
- Time management books or courses can be very effective in developing skills and habits.
- Stress management techniques can be learnt from books.
- Learn to do things for enjoyment and learn to enjoy the things you do
- Check with others what they expect and admire in terms of professional standards of behaviour.
- Examine honestly your work-life balance. What do you do to relax? How often?
- Try to find out what barriers there are to you achieving success

Summary

Well done. You have just completed the first part of a comprehensive review of your personal skills, namely your ability to manage yourself. In the next chapter we will look at communication skills.

Family 2: Communication

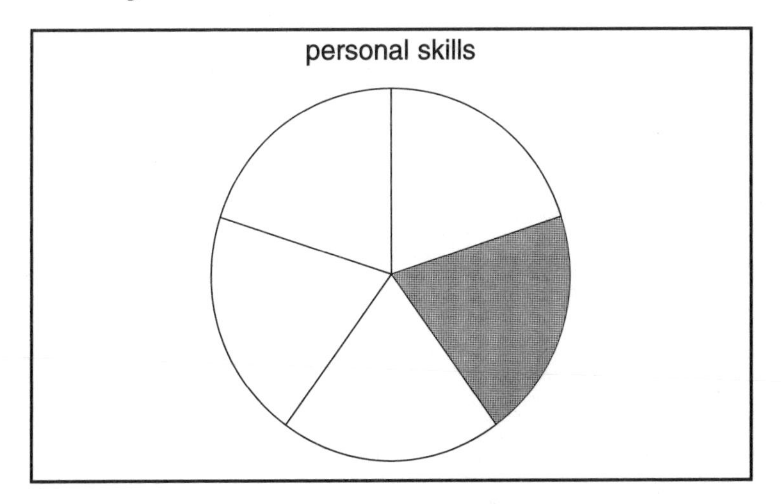

For many people, communication would come first on their list of life skills required to thrive in social or working environments. This is so much so that we hardly need to question why this family of skills is deemed to be so important.

At bottom, the reasons centre around the fact that life and work are primarily social. They involve interaction with other people. Work, particularly, involves the exchange of various sorts of information between individuals, departments and other categories of people.

Yet communication is no simple matter. There is no one single factor or aptitude that underlies this family of skills. It is possible to be good at one aspect of communication and poor at another. Think of people who can write clearly, fluently and even elegantly and yet can be tongue-tied and uncomfortable when trying to communicate on a face-to-face basis.

Nonetheless, our ability to contribute in the area of communications is one of the primary ways that we are judged by others. And this is particularly so in the world of work.

Family map

This family of competencies looks like this:

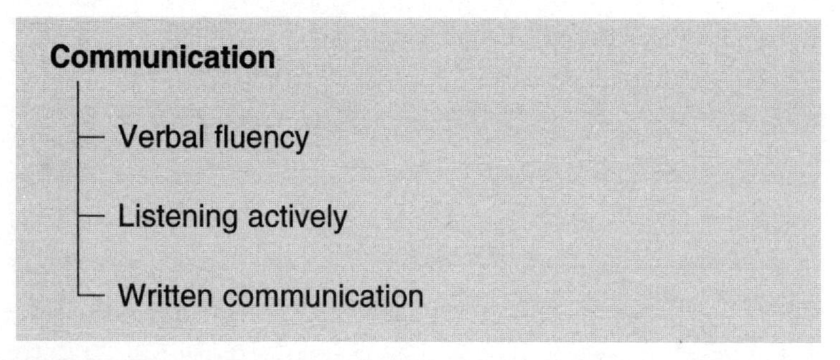

Role model
Many public figures are highly skilled communicators. Politicians can be distinguished by their ability to articulate simple but powerful messages and to communicate them with skill and belief.

Think of a good communicator that you admire. Identify two or three things at which they are particularly skilled. Do these account for their competence in this area?

Verbal fluency

Overview
Verbal fluency is about being a good talker. That much is obvious. However, it is also about much more than that. We all know people who talk and talk, monopolising

conversations, ignoring us and our needs with their own selfish need to rattle on regardless. This implies that as well as the things that they do, equally, there are things that they are failing to do or are doing badly.

The talking part involves us being able to form ideas clearly and to be able to express them simply, but with impact. But being articulate is just one aspect of the skill. In addition, there are other important aspects, such as:

- choosing the right time and the right place
- enhancing speech with non-verbal behaviour (body and voice tone)
- responding to the needs and interests of others
- reading and influencing the mood of the conversation
- being able to speak in various contexts.

At work we may need to be skilled at talking in a variety of contexts – ranging from formal presentations to one-to-one situations, as well as more social types of conversation. Of course, as individuals, we may not be equally skilled in all of these areas.

Positive indicators
Good talkers:

- generate interest from others
- use humour appropriately
- are able to articulate and put across ideas
- elicit responses
- encourage two-way conversation
- display positive non-verbal behaviour.

Negative indicators
Bad talkers:

- bore people
- dominate conversation
- cut across others or interrupt constantly
- use annoying mannerisms, such as 'like' or 'y'know'.

Illustration

He was one of those people that as soon as he came into a room, all eyes were on him. When he started talking, it was almost impossible not to pay attention. He just had a way of engaging your interest, and keeping you enthralled.

A senior manager, speaking of his own Managing Director

Listening actively

Overview
Everybody understands the notion of listening. Most people also rate themselves as good listeners. Actually, good listeners are few and far between. This is because good listening is a high-level skill that needs developing.

The key word here is active. Listening is not a passive activity – you have to work at it. Many of those people who think they are good listeners are those who equate listening with taking in information. But as well as this we also need to involve ourselves. This means:

- trying to grasp the meaning of what is said
- demonstrating that you understand
- checking your interpretation and reflecting it back
- paying attention to emotional as well as logical content
- using verbal and non-verbal techniques to gain rapport and keep the conversation flowing.

Indicators

Good listeners:

- gain rapport easily
- acknowledge what is said
- don't interrupt or cut across
- follow the logic and flow of the conversation
- display comfortable and fluent non-verbal behaviour.

Written communication

Overview

There are many situations in life and at work where we have to express ourselves in writing. Whether this be in the form of letters, reports, memos or, increasingly, in e-mail, it is a basic life and work skill. Literacy is one of the key foundations of our school education – and for good reason.

In work, communicating well in writing has a whole range of advantages. It can obviously improve communication and so aids efficiency and performance. It can help to improve or maintain relationships and even motivation for others, when skilfully used. Finally, it can enhance our reputation and professionalism.

Indicators

Good writers:

- use appropriate format
- communicate when necessary
- write simple, clear and accurate text
- can express and communicate ideas with impact
- use appropriate language for the purpose and audience
- can spell and use grammar correctly.

Illustration

The company brief used to read like a technical manual that was passed around for managers to use at their discretion. Problem was, everybody used to use it in different ways and added their own interpretation. The briefings were awful. Now it is done as a PowerPoint presentation. Everybody gets the same message, but the presentation is so much clearer and readable. It's made a real difference to people's understanding of what's going on and why, and they feel more positive about it.

Manager in a pharmaceutical company

Assessing your communication skills

?

Test Yourself

Now it is time to assess yourself, as you did for the last family. For each competency, rate yourself on a scale of 1 to 5. Ask a colleague to rate you too. Then, work out your own average score, as well as the third party's average score, for your performance in this family as a whole.

Verbal fluency

Low: Disinclined to engage in conversation. Have difficulty expressing ideas in words. Lack confidence in conversational or social contexts.

High: Enjoy conversation. Hold an audience. Express ideas clearly and with impact in conversation. Highly articulate. Confident in speaking to groups.

Role model	expert	competent	inconsistent	poor
5	4	3	2	1

self-assessment ☐ third-party assessment ☐

Listening actively

Low: Appear intent on own agenda. Talk more than they listen. Don't respond to clues and themes of others. Cut across and interrupts.

High: Keep the interest of other parties. Allow others to 'open up'. Acknowledge and respond to statements of others. Confident verbal and non-verbal skills. Able to maintain flow of conversation.

Role model	expert	competent	inconsistent	poor
5	4	3	2	1

self-assessment ☐ third-party assessment ☐

Written communication

Low: Rarely commit ideas and propositions to writing. Use poor construction, complex language and poor structure in written documents.

High: Use appropriate format for written communications. Sets out ideas clearly and simply in good English. Use logical structure. Communicate with impact.

Role model	expert	competent	inconsistent	poor
5	4	3	2	1

self-assessment ☐ third-party assessment ☐

Average score for communication:

self-assessment ☐ third-party assessment ☐

Developing communication skills

Developing the ability to express your ideas clearly involves a number of things. Firstly, check that your non-verbal behaviour is helping you to communicate rather than the opposite. Check your posture and body language is positive. Try to 'hear' yourself. Do you vary your voice tone and inject enthusiasm and other positive emotions into it? Is your voice too strident and loud? Or is your tone flat and boring?

Next, think about the messages that you want to convey in the various contexts that you communicate. In more formal settings, such as presentations, have you worked out the messages that you wish to convey, or do you just ramble? In more social settings, check that you are keeping people's interest. Do you give them plenty of chance to talk and respond to what you have said? Do you check that they have understood what you have said? Do you pay attention to mood and emotion as well as to pure content?

By gaining feedback and information on all of these factors, it will help you to understand your own strengths and shortcomings. From there, it is a short move to doing something about it.

Speaking and listening really require you to understand what it is that you are not doing well. Active listening takes practice, as it is hard work. Try setting yourself the task of keeping someone talking with the minimum intervention from yourself. Ensure that you give them enough clues that:

- you have heard
- you understand
- you are interested to know more.

With verbal fluency, getting better sometimes involves developing the habit of thinking a bit more before you commit to saying anything. Try to reduce the key messages of what you want to say to very simple, single sentences. For important conversations, you can even try to rehearse these before you try them on others.

For written communication, there are many books and courses available that set out robust principles that are easy to learn and follow.

Summary

After completing this chapter, you should already be beginning to gain hard data on some of the key factors that contribute to your success in life, especially if you have used other people to provide an independent assessment.

In the next chapter, we will look at the third family, relationships.

Family 3: Relationships

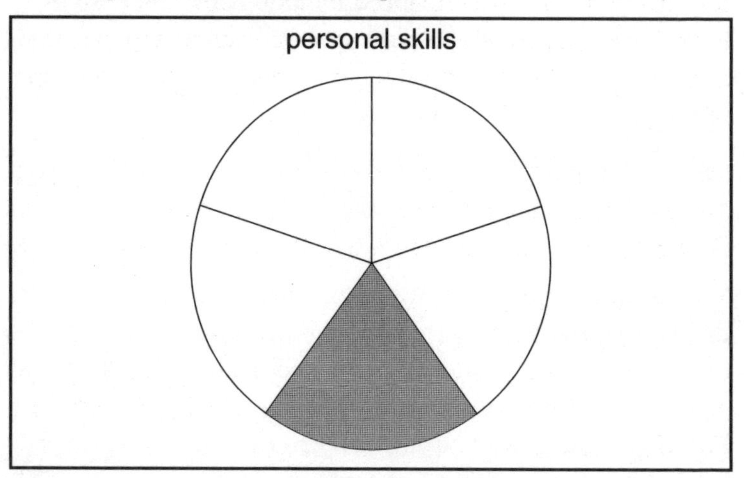

Relationships are at the root of our functioning as social beings. We have basic needs as humans to relate to other people. To function in society we need to be able to develop relationships with diverse people, from family and friends to the shopkeeper and the bus conductor.

To complicate things, relationships at work also take many forms. Just think of the many different types of relationship involved:

- friends
- colleagues
- line managers
- management in general
- subordinates
- team members
- customers
- suppliers.

Also, the media through which relationships are now conducted, have been enhanced by technology. Increasingly, many of these relationships are being conducted via technological means – telephone, e-mail and so on.

Different conventions apply to many of these relationships. Yet, to thrive and be successful we have to be able to establish, build and maintain all of these relationships.

As well as our social needs for affinity, relationships also affect other psychological areas. We are most of us concerned at how other people see us. Our relationships are a part of how we see ourselves in the world and so they affect our own self-image and self-esteem.

Everyone is different and there are as many ways of dealing with other people as there are people. Our style will suit some people but it may not suit everyone. Not all of our professional relationships will be good. Not all will be as strong or intimate as the friendships that we form outside of work.

The impression we give to others about ourselves is done very early on in a relationship. It has been claimed, for instance, that in interviews, an interviewer will make up his/her mind about us in as little as 30 seconds. That does suggest that in a working context, we should try to ensure that even the earliest impression we give to others is positive.

Family map

This family of competencies looks like this:

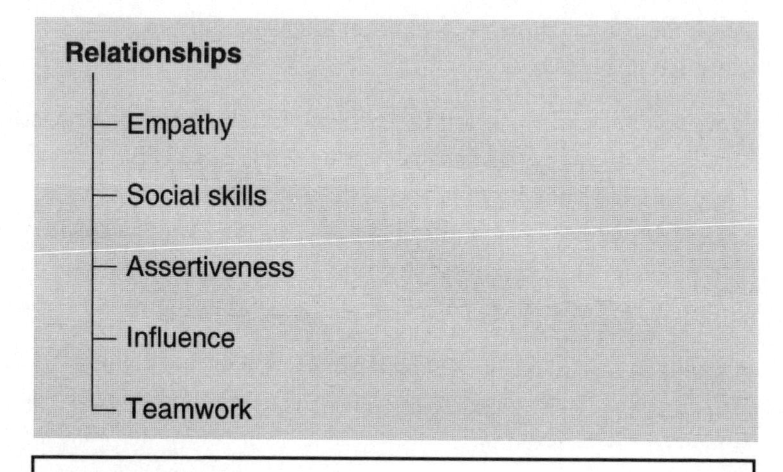

Illustration

In a survey of HR managers, the Institute of Management (September 2000) found that '93% considered important or very important the so-called "soft skills" of teamworking and interpersonal skills – essential requirements of the service-oriented economy.'

Empathy

Overview

This is described as: 'an ability to see into another's mind and heart and so reach a full and sympathetic understanding of his [sic] thought, feeling or experience.'

In other words, it is the ability to see (and feel) the world through the eyes of another person. Firstly, this means we need to be alert to the feelings of the other person. Secondly, we need to acknowledge that we have noticed them. Finally, we have to accept those feelings in their own right, without dismissing, rationalising away or contradicting them.

It is particularly important to do this when the other person is dealing with difficult or overwhelming emotions. This can happen when they have sadness, disappointment or even grief in their lives. It can also happen when we have to deliver bad news. The skilled person is able to steer a way between being honesty (to the point of bluntness) and avoidance.

This level of sensitivity is a high-level skill and is not easy to acquire, but we can improve if we sensitise ourselves to the needs of others.

Indicators
Good emphathisers:

- are able to understand the emotions of others
- are sensitive to the needs of others
- cope with a wide range of emotions and experiences
- display congruent non-verbal behaviour.

Social skills

Overview
This is the diverse set of skills in which we apply ourselves to the business of initiating, building, maintaining and enhancing our relationships in life and work. In the working context, these are our personal skills applied to relating to others.

As we have already pointed out, there is a huge range of types and levels of relationships that operate in life and particularly in working life. Some are more formal than others. Some are nearer to friendships or even partnerships. Some are voluntary and are based on shared interest or 'chemistry', while others exist because they have to (such as customer relationships).

In addition to the deeply human and personal aspects of relationships, such as the empathy dealt with above, there are some requirements that come purely from our professional relationship to each other. In these cases other issues come into play. These include:

- informing – telling people what they need to know, keeping them up to date
- consulting – seeking opinion and input from those with a vested interest in what we do or are about to do
- agreeing – achieving consensus or approval among interested parties for decisions, projects, initiatives and so on
- checking – eliciting other perspectives; checking understanding; clarifying interpretations
- respecting – the positions and needs of others, even if they are different to our own.

A final element of social skills is sociability. As a person, are you at ease in the company of others? It is important to say that, although sociability is influenced by our own introversion-extraversion tendencies, it does not mean that introverts cannot be sociable and cannot make strong personal relationships. Neither is it related to being loud and talkative. It is more a question of taking time and interest in others, showing a willingness to spend time with them and an interest in their needs.

Indicators

People with good social skills:

- are comfortable in the company of others
- are sociable
- are good company
- have a wide range of relationships.

Assertiveness

Overview

The working environment can be a formidable personal challenge for many people. We all have our own inhibitions, perhaps shyness or a compliant attitude learned over many years from family, friends and school. People do get socialised into not standing up for themselves, because this behaviour is interpreted as difficult or 'stroppy'. As a result, some people develop a tendency to back down from unpleasantness or conflict. This may lead us to feel that we can only gain the approval of others by being nice or compliant and we don't always stand up for ourselves as well as we might want to.

Our ability and inclination to give a good account of ourselves in social situations is also related to our self-esteem and confidence.

To add to this, organisations have many other ways to intimidate us. There is plenty to misunderstand and be confused about. There are hierarchies to defer to and respect. We will deal with colleagues who know more than us or who are more experienced in their own field. Nonetheless, we are required to talk to them on an even footing.

We may also be more inclined to be assertive is some areas (for instance with subordinates) but not with others (for instance with senior managers). Some people may find it more difficult or easy to be assertive with particular groups – for instance, the opposite sex. In thinking of your own self assessment, don't just apply a global criterion, but try to differentiate.

So, how do we balance the fulfilment of our own needs with those of others? Conflict will always occur in any field of human relations. Whether it be family, social circles, football teams, school governing bodies, there will always be clashes between individuals. These can come about for many reasons:

- misunderstanding
- disagreement about objectives or decisions
- different interpretations, perspectives, world views or cultures
- perceived or actual threats to vested interest
- clash of personality or style.

Whenever such conflicts or differences occur, we, as individuals, have choices as to how we tackle them. For some, their primary or default approach or strategy is to ignore the conflict, while others will seek to avoid the conflict by giving in to the needs of others.

However, we can pay a high price for lacking in assertiveness. We may fail to stand up for our own interests. We may be less effective socially and in work. We may actually finish up being less interesting or less respected by our colleagues.

More robust approaches might involve tackling the conflict in a confrontational or even brutal way. This might have a short-term advantage ('I win'), but of course this might be at the expense of other benefits. For instance, it may harm the relationship for the future. Or it could be that the ideas or position rejected might have been better.

You should also be aware of not just how much and when you are challenging, but how you go about it. Some people have developed the talent of being able to challenge without being overly personal or breaking the relationship.

Assertion involves being able to say no to unreasonable demands. It also involves 'standing our ground'. That is, being able to put our own case – our interests, our point of view and so on. In some cases, it can involve having the courage of our convictions.

Indicators

Assertive people:

- can say no
- can put their own case or point of view, or advocate their own agenda and legitimate interests
- comply or conform by choice rather than habit
- can challenge positions or decisions
- can separate the issue from the person
- can listen to the other point of view
- compromise or seek agreement when appropriate
- can mediate in conflict between other people
- match their approach to the situation appropriately
- can 'forgive and forget'

- give negative feedback in a constructive manner.

Influence

Overview

What is influence? Influence is the ability to affect or change the behaviour or opinions of other people. It involves questions such as :

- Do people listen to our position and ideas?
- Do they act on what we say?
- In negotiations and discussions, can we set out a case and change the strategy or decisions of others?

Influencing, then, involves a number of underlying components. A basic foundation is clearly around communication skills. Can we articulate ideas? Can we demonstrate understanding of key issues? Can we communicate a position, idea or decision? Related to this is the notion of being able to listen, understand and acknowledge the position of other people. It is difficult to influence other people if we can't communicate and convince them that we understand their interests and needs.

Other foundations for influence include:

- strength and attractiveness of our ideas and vision – do people know where we stand?
- credibility – do people have reason and evidence to believe what we say and thus to respect our opinions?

- logic – our ability to persuade or convince by logical and rational argument
- connectivity/networking – do we have strong relationships with opinion formers, the 'movers and shakers'?
- context – do we have and demonstrate an understanding of the basic issues and forces operating within our own context? Do we know what's going on in our own world?

These are all aspects that go to make up strong influence.

Indicators
Strong influencers:

- understands key issues
- communicate relevant information
- have personal credibility by virtue of knowledge and/or skill
- use communication skills to set out arguments and to convince others of ideas and courses of action
- seek views of others
- promote and lobby for ideas and propositions.

Teamwork

Overview
Teamwork has been a creed in management for as long as any of us can remember. There is good reason for this. At the most basic, it is because of the notion of synergy:

$2 + 2 = 5$

You can get more from a team than from the sum of the

efforts of the individuals involved. Emphasis on teamwork is not just about efficiency and effectiveness. It also has a strong sociological and psychological aspect. Teamwork has a cultural dimension. For many organisations, working co-operatively and sharing are part of the way that they like to do things. Working in teams satisfies many of our individual human needs – for affinity, involvement, control, participation and so on.

It should be said that to work in this way is not the exclusive invention of business and organisational theorists. It is a perfectly natural human way of going about our lives. Look in your own personal and social life and think of all of the teams or co-operative communities to which you belong. Management thinking on this subject has also been influenced by what we know of teams from other domains, such as the world of sport.

What research has shown, however, is that people contribute different things to teams, based on their own personal preferences and strengths. Some contribute leadership and direction setting (in the Belbin team role framework, these are called shaper and chairman). Others contribute ideas, intelligence and information, and yet others contribute to the work of the team and the completion of tasks and projects.

Here, we are focusing on the more general notion of contribution to the work of teams – being a good team player. So what do good team players do?

Indicators
Good team players:

- involve others in their activities, and in turn get involved in group and co-operative activities
- share knowledge and ideas
- accept their share of responsibility
- cultivate relationships
- contribute appropriately to their role (in terms of task and in terms of team role (see above)
- support other team members
- co-operate with others in activities
- give feedback to others
- promote a positive and supportive climate
- show skill in resolving conflicts and tensions
- encourage others to contribute according to their strengths
- can balance own agenda and needs with shared objectives and needs.

Assessing your relationships skills

?

Test Yourself

Now it is time to assess yourself, as you did for the last family. For each competency, rate yourself on a scale of 1 to 5. Ask a colleague to rate you too. The, work out your own average score, as well as the third-party's average score, for your performance in this family as a whole.

Empathy

Low: Can appear cold and unfeeling. Lack sensitivity. Find it difficult to demonstrate understanding of the needs of others.

High: Emotionally secure and mature. Generate warmth and sympathetic understanding of other people. Demonstrate sensitivity to the needs of others.

Role model	expert	competent	inconsistent	poor
5	4	3	2	1

self-assessment ☐ third-party assessment ☐

Social skills

Low: Uneasy in the company of others. Lack skill and consideration in dealing with others.

High: At ease in relationships. Highly sociable. Involve and inform others. Popular and seen to be good company.

Role model	expert	competent	inconsistent	poor
5	4	3	2	1

self-assessment ☐ third-party assessment ☐

Influence

Low: Have few or poor relationships with key players and decision-makers. Don't set out credible opinions on important matters. Don't engage or contribute in discussions on decisions. Keep themselves to themselves. Finds it difficult to articulate ideas, arguments or strategies. Have low visibility.

High: Act as ambassadors for department/project/function. Viewed as expert in own area. Maintain network relationships and information exchange with other key players, both internally and externally. Are seen to 'know what's going on'. Are consulted on major issues. Have high visibility.

Role model	expert	competent	inconsistent	poor
5	4	3	2	1

self-assessment ☐ third-party assessment ☐

Teamwork

Low: Low involvement in group activities. Make little or negative contribution in group situations. Pursue own agenda at expense of team. Disinclined to share with or support others.

High: Enjoy co-operative activities. Share knowledge and ideas readily. Make positive contributions in group situations. Support other team members.

Role model	expert	competent	inconsistent	poor
5	4	3	2	1

self-assessment ☐ third-party assessment ☐

Assertiveness

Low: Avoid disagreement and conflict or back down in confrontations. Resort too quickly to aggression or an 'I win, you lose' strategy. Cause of discomfort for others.

High: Able to stand their ground and say no where appropriate. Able to separate people from issues. Can deal with conflict in a mature manner. Engineer 'win-win' options and outcomes where possible.

Role model	expert	competent	inconsistent	poor
5	4	3	2	1

self-assessment ☐ third-party assessment ☐

Average score for relationships:

self-assessment ☐ third-party assessment ☐

Developing relationship skills

Let us take a more qualitative approach to thinking about this family of competencies. Firstly, draw up a list of adjectives that you think apply to yourself when considered in a social context (co-operative, loyal etc.). Ask a colleague (or a few), who knows you well, to do the same. Attributes of positive relationships that it could be helpful to think about include:

- fairness
- being consistent
- loyalty
- honesty
- sense of humour
- warmth
- sympathy/empathy
- openness
- putting people at ease.

By comparing these lists you will not only begin to understand how others see you, but you will also appreciate how near your self-perception is to the perception of others. Nowhere is this more important than when thinking about relationships. This, together with your ratings for this family of skills, will give you some very clear ideas about where you need to develop.

Other development ideas can derive from answering a few key questions :

- Do I show enough interest in other people?
- Do I take time to chat to people? Do I ask or know enough about their interests, their feelings?
- Do I come across as warm and sympathetic? If not, is this because I am moody? Or perhaps because I treat people with suspicion?

- Do I show respect for the ideas and feelings of other people?
- What do I contribute in a team environment? Is this contribution visible? Is it ever acknowledged?
- Am I seen as overly compliant? Or alternatively, am I seen as being unnecessarily challenging or even hostile? What do I do that makes me seem that way?
- Do I face up to problems? Do I tackle difficult situations in a fair, respectful and even-handed manner?

Like much in life, good things only develop with work and effort. Overall, you should be asking if you pay enough attention to the needs of others. Relationships need an investment of time. If you do not spend the time, then good relationships cannot develop. If you feel you do invest the time, then there may be something about the way you are dealing with people that gets in the way of good relationships.

Many people can and do develop certain kinds of relationships effectively, but others cannot. Some people treat subordinates less well than they should. Others find it difficult to make quality relationships with authority figures. This needs some introspection and examination.

Family 4: Thinking skills

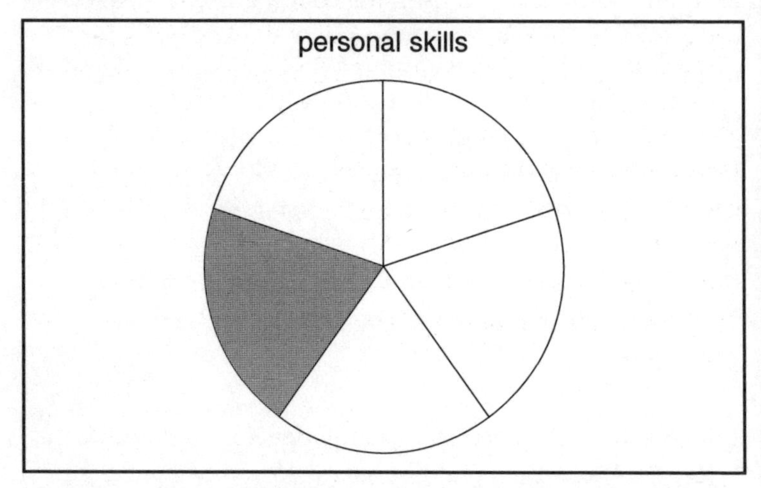

There are many qualities required to 'get on' in the world and be successful. Parents, schools and the education system in general probably tried to convince you that getting qualifications and good educational standards was a prize for intelligent people. There is some justification in this. Intelligence is indeed related to success in life and career. Of course, it is not by any means the only factor and there are plenty of examples of clever people who do not achieve, and, of course, of less clever people who are extremely successful.

Nonetheless, thinking skills are highly prized and rewarded in most areas of life and work. There are many reasons for this. A look around at the modern economy and world of work will give some immediate clues. It wasn't that long ago when the primary skills required for most adults were physical, as the world of work was based on manufacturing and making things. We are now in the information age and the rules have changed. In our current economy, knowledge is itself the commodity in such a lot of organisations. In these circumstances, the key skills for dealing with knowledge and information are thinking and analytic skills.

In addition, organisations themselves change and staff become more empowered – being enabled and required to make their own decisions and to change and adapt at a rapid pace. Therefore, the skills involved in processing information, solving problems and making decisions become ever more important.

At the same time, this does not mean that the world is only fit for Mensa members. It is true that organisations do pay attention to our underlying cognitive skills (fluid intelligence, which you can read about in *Test Your Aptitude and Ability*). However, if this is the 'raw material' that we as individuals have to work with, it is equally important that we are able to apply those abilities to the learning of practical and work-focused skills.

Family map

This family of competencies looks like this:

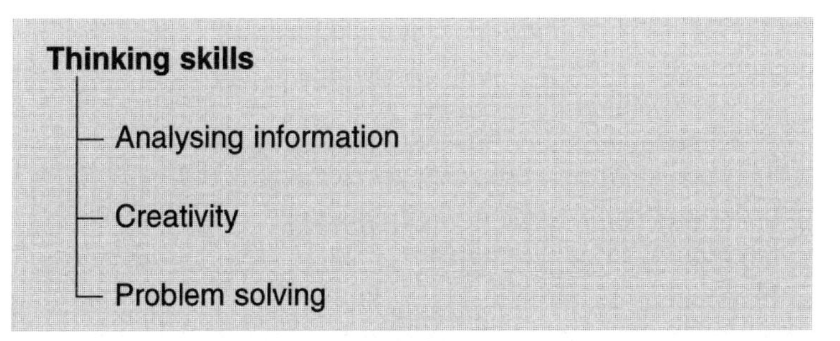

Illustration

The value employers place upon the basic skills of literacy and numeracy is once again reinforced by the findings of this survey. Ninety per cent considered them important or very important [. . .] They also placed a high premium – 95% – on communication skills and problem-solving and analytic thinking.

Institute of Management press release summarising a survey of HR managers, September 2000

Analysing information

Overview

This is really the core competency within this family, as it involves the underlying skills for analysing information in various forms. This is the information-processing aspect of this family. It involves applying a good level of cognitive skill to information in the working environment.

Indicators

Analytical people:

- have awareness of the environment
- seek information and ideas from a variety of sources
- assimilate complex data and ideas
- identify relationships and patterns in complex information
- identify key issues and draw conclusions and inferences
- obtain information and intelligence
- draw correct or appropriate conclusions based on data provided

- identify links between apparently unrelated data
- discriminate between conflicting or alternative arguments.

Creativity

Overview

Most of us admire creativity in people when we come across it in any walk of life. Creative thinking provides the 'spark' or the special insight that leads to innovation or developments in every aspect of human activity. Think of things that you admire in areas that interest you such as:

- science
- the arts
- politics
- sport and human performance
- the media.

We can think of specific innovations that involved someone somewhere thinking in a different way, or in somehow breaking boundaries. It is this unusualness or uniqueness that so often characterises creative thinking. We call it 'thinking out of the box', which indicates that it is so often not obvious and not derived by purely linear logical thinking. So not only do we admire the people who can contribute to such developments, but they are vitally important in moving along human culture and achievement.

Of course, in the business environment, creativity is also important in helping to harness technology to products and services and to aid competition.

There is a certain kind of creativity (with a big 'C') that is the territory of the genius. These are the Mozarts, the Leonardos and the Einsteins. Very few of us can aspire to that kind of creativity. However, there is a different kind of creativity (with a little 'c') that we can all access. In our own worlds, we can contribute novel ideas, insights, suggestions for improvements, solutions to problems and so on. This kind of creativity still involves some or all of the following indicators.

Indicators

Creative people:

- have deep knowledge of their own subject or area
- can view things from unusual perspectives
- come up with novel ideas or approaches
- can ideate (generate ideas to order)
- are open to new ideas and experiences
- take risks
- don't mind going against the flow
- dare to be different.

Problem-solving

Overview

This is using our thinking and analytic skills, applying them to the tackling of real problems and issues. It therefore involves the cognitive and the very pragmatic. Our ability to solve problems, then, is a balance between these two aspects:

- our underlying thinking and reasoning skills
- our knowledge of the real world and the judgement we apply to it.

This balance is important. You may be able to think of very bright and intelligent people that you know, who are nonetheless very poor at tackling real issues, and who make unfortunate decisions.

Indicators

Good problem-solvers:

- gather and select appropriate information
- sort out the important from the less important issues
- take an ordered and structured approach to dealing with situations
- generate practical options and solutions
- evaluate options
- make sound decisions – even in uncertain circumstances
- evaluate the impact and consequences of decisions.

Assessing your thinking skills

?

Test Yourself

Now it is time to assess yourself, as you did for the last family. For each competency, rate yourself on a scale of 1 to 5. Ask a colleague to rate you too. Then, work out your own average score, as well as the third-party's average score, for your performance in this family as a whole.

Analysing information

Low: Get confused when confronted with complex information. Draw unwarranted conclusions. Uncomfortable with conceptual information. Fail to spot patterns or trends.

High: Seek out and understand key information. Make sense of complex information. Conceptually fluent.

Role model expert competent inconsistent poor

5 4 3 2 1

self-assessment ☐ third-party assessment ☐

Creativity

Low: Respond in predictable ways to challenges. Have difficulty with new ideas. Reluctant to think radically.

High: Always have new ideas or approaches. Able to 'think out of the box'. Challenge assumptions.

Role model expert competent inconsistent poor

5 4 3 2 1

self-assessment ☐ third-party assessment ☐

Problem-solving

Low: Haphazard in approach. Make poor decisions based on incomplete information.

High: Able to obtain and organise appropriate information. Have an ordered and methodical approach to dealing with problems. Evaluate options. Make sound decisions.

Role model expert competent inconsistent poor

5 4 3 2 1

self-assessment ☐ third-party assessment ☐

Average/overall score for problem solving

self-assessment ☐ third-party assessment ☐

Other ways of assessing your thinking skills

Because it relates to ability, many aspects of this underlying skill can be measured by objective testing. Information-processing skills vary according to our preferences for different kinds of information. Our underlying ability can usually be classified into one of three:

- verbal ability and reasoning
- numerical ability and reasoning
- abstract or diagrammatic reasoning.

These can be tested by psychometric ability tests and if you have undergone these, you should have a good idea of your repertoire of abilities. If not, you can get some idea from your level of educational attainment. For instance, if you are a trained and qualified systems analyst, you are likely to have a higher than normal abstract reasoning ability. Similar arguments apply to attainment in English or humanities subjects, or to mathematics or quantitative ones.

How well you apply these abilities is really only tested in relation to work or life achievements and experiences.

Developing thinking skills

Overview

Thinking skills can be compared to physical fitness. That is, we are born with a certain underlying capability or a set of limits and it is difficult to alter this. We have also developed over a lifetime a certain level of 'fitness'. However, just as with our physical capability, it is possible to maximise the benefit of what we have. Remember too, that it is estimated that all of us use only a fraction of the capability of our brains.

The key to getting better at applying our abilities in life and work contexts lies in learning to use what we have better. The key to that is practice. It is well worthwhile looking at the psychometric approach to measuring your aptitudes and abilities. The title *Test Your Aptitude and Ability*, in this series will help you here. There are also many books available to help you practise and develop specific aspects of aptitude and ability.

In terms of applying these to real-life situations, a good way to develop and practise your approach is to examine and reflect on some key experiences. Take some real problem situations or decisions you have been involved in. Try reviewing them in the following way :

- Did I obtain all the information I needed?
- Did I use it to get a complete grasp and understanding of the situation?
- Did I approach the situation in an ordered and methodical manner?
- Did I generate and evaluate various options?
- Did I anticipate the consequences of my decisions and actions?
- Were the outcomes favourable?
- What could I have done better?

In this way, you will begin to learn more from your experiences and to widen your repertoire of skills.

Family 5: Getting things done

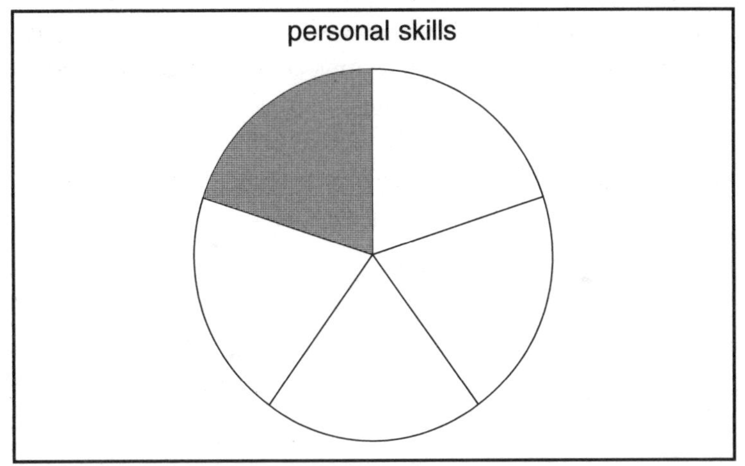

This one really poses a question: do we accept the world and our lot – as it is? Or do we 'take the bull by the horns' and set out to achieve what we want? It is really about focusing on and achieving results.

In all aspects of life we are likely to appreciate and applaud those who can get things done. To get things done we have to be able to turn ambitions and dreams to reality by initiating action and seeing it through.

People who do this are likely to:

- know what they want
- focus on outcomes and results – to set high but achievable goals
- be able to move from thought to action
- be able to complete on projects, actions and initiatives
- have a track record of achievement and of getting what they want.

However, there is also some subtlety associated with this family. In a complex world, we need to be able to do this in demanding and ever-shifting circumstances. We need to be able to juggle – to keep all the balls in the air. Working and operating in pressured and complex environments is a balancing act that most of us have to achieve. Achieving results, while our focus of attention is spread over many competing priorities, is difficult to master.

Similarly, this has to be done while the goals are always shifting. It is for these reasons that the multi-tasking and adapting to change competencies are included in this family.

Family map

This family of competencies looks like this:

Getting things done

- Focus on achievement
- Multi-tasking
- Adapting to change

Illustration

Fortunately, there was someone in the lab who kept telling me I was a square peg in a round hole and that spurred me on to prove myself. I have this bloody-minded perversity so if someone tells me I can't do something, I carry on doing it.

Susan Greenfield, Professor of Pharmacology at Oxford University.

Focus on achievement

Overview

This competency focuses on the ability to pay attention to and deliver recognisable outcomes. People who score high on this strand tend to set high goals and achieve them. They focus on the completion of tasks, rather than immersion in a task for its own sake.

> The best was for me to stop analysing and to start implementing. They were right because you can analyse something to death and get a perfect strategy only to find you're too late.
>
> *Nick Reilly, chairman and MD of Vauxhall Motors, on being asked the best advice anyone had given him.*

What the illustration shows is that it is very important not only to set goals and strategies but to turn them into reality. The best thinking in the world is of little value if it is not acted on. This in turn implies that important aspects of this strand are the ability to:

- set goals and targets (to know where the goalposts are)
- move from thinking to doing
- stick with something despite setbacks.

Indicators

Achievers:

- have track record – achievements are usually publicly acknowledged
- have ambition

- have vision – can articulate future achievements
- make plans and review progress
- have determination to stick to the task
- take control
- favour action
- set high goals
- meet deadlines
- are decisive.

Multi-tasking

In a complex world, we need to be able to pay attention to more than one thing at a time. In addition, we need to be able to be involved in a range of activities that run in parallel and overlap. We need to apply various skills in different projects and at different times. We need to be able to juggle.

If we look at the range of possible roles we are required to carry out, we may be:

- a mother to children
- a wife to a husband
- a friend
- a confidante
- a mentor
- a younger sister
- an organiser for the PTA
- an expert at work.

Life can be very complex when we have to be able to switch fluently from role to role many times in a day and in a week. This requires a substantial amount of flexibility and adaptability.

Indicators
Jugglers:

- can cope with competing demands
- prioritise activities
- have stamina and drive
- balance work and life
- can switch attention quickly when necessary
- cope well in a crisis
- are in control of their own time and workload.

Adapting to change

Overview
One thing we do know about the world – particularly the world of work – is that tomorrow will be different from today. It is a very important lifeskill and workskill that we are able to adapt to the changes that will happen to us. It is easy to think of the transitions that we pass through in our lives:

- ageing and maturing
- achieving qualifications
- buying or moving house
- having children
- losing family, friends
- illness, and so on.

These kinds of transitions are mirrored in our working lives:

- take-overs, mergers and acquisitions
- changing jobs
- promotions
- annual reviews
- new customers and products
- new technology
- new systems and procedures
- new staff to recruit, train, develop
- new colleagues and bosses
- outsourcing
- downsizing.

Because of the rapid pace of change in organisations, the skills to cope and to thrive in such circumstances are highly valued. In fact, in many organisations, they are a prerequisite. In order to cope, we need to lose our fear of change and develop our ability to adapt and prosper.

Indicators

Chameleons:

- understand need for change
- have positive orientation
- embrace new experiences
- learn new skills
- adapt to changing circumstances and priorities
- experiment with new ideas
- identify opportunities for improvements in performance
- develop strategies to cope with future changes.

Assessing your getting things done skills

?

Test Yourself

Now it is time to assess yourself, as you did for the last family. For each competency, rate yourself on a scale of 1 to 5. Ask a colleague to rate you too. Then, work out your own average score, as well as the third-party's average score, for your performance in this family as a whole.

Focus on achievement

Low: Find it difficult to articulate outcomes and goals. Take too long to make decisions. Content to 'roll with the punches'. Lack ambition and drive.

High: Recognised as achievers with track records of results to show. Strong 'can-do' streak. Show determination in getting results and successful conclusions. Know the difference between winning and losing.

Role model	expert	competent	inconsistent	poor
5	4	3	2	1

self-assessment ☐ third-party assessment ☐

Multi-tasking

Low: Panic in a crisis. Reactive management. Unable to keep up or get on top of events. Retreat when faced with a range of challenges.

High: In control of events. Deal with multiple competing demands. Good time management.

Role model	expert	competent	inconsistent	poor
5	4	3	2	1

self-assessment ☐ third-party assessment ☐

Adapting to change

Low: Appear inflexible. 'Stuck in the mud'. Negative or pessimistic orientation. Perceive change as a threat.

High: Positive orientation and openness to new experiences. Flexible, with a degree of spontaneity. Future-oriented and able to plan ahead.

Role model	expert	competent	inconsistent	poor
5	4	3	2	1

self-assessment ☐ third-party assessment ☐

Average score for getting things done

self-assessment ☐ third-party assessment ☐

Developing getting things done skills

There are a range of underlying skills and abilities associated with this family. And as with most applied skills, these can be developed and enhanced over time. On the whole, they are not of the book-learning type of skills. They are the kinds of skills that are developed by examining our approach, by mature reflection and by developing new habits.

These skills include:

- making decisions
- breaking down goals into discrete actions
- planning and organising
- prioritising.

These skills are balanced by other factors. The first of these involves our basic orientations. These are quite deeply ingrained for most of us. You can get some clues about them by looking at your personal preferences, using a psychometric test. They are covered in *Test Your Personality* in this series.

Such basic orientations include whether you are positive or negative, optimistic or pessimistic. They also include your basic approach to control in your life (intrinsic or extrinsic). Are you forward-looking and future-oriented or are you rooted in the present?

Although it is difficult to change these substantially, it is extremely useful to be self-aware. It may help you to understand how you come across to other people.

Another relevant factor is the set of habits that we have developed over a lifetime to cope with change and complexity in the world. Take some examples:

- Do you back away from a challenge?
- Do you panic in a crisis?
- Do you have a tendency to 'let the future take care of itself'?

By seeking feedback on these issues and by looking in detail at how you have responded in times of challenge, you should get clear ideas about your own habits. You will then be able to assess what is good about them, what is less useful and what you can work on to improve.

More issues that affect personal success

Introduction

So far, our logical approach may have given you the impression that personal effectiveness can be measured simply by mapping yourself onto a list of personal skills.

Unfortunately, life is not so simple. In reality, each of these personal skills are complex, multi-faceted and changeable aspects of behaviour. Their impact has to be placed within the much wider context of the total package you offer to the outside world, but also within the context in which you operate. We would like to turn now to consider three of the factors that will profoundly affect your personal success, namely:

- Behavioural roles
- Cultural models
- Motivation

Behavioural roles

In the process model we presented at the start of this book, we identified the inputs as personal skills or qualities, and the outputs as functional skills or the proven ability to achieve results in the workplace. The truth is that all of these qualities interface with your environment through the behaviours you show when interacting with others. In other words, the processes, which are business skills or behaviours, are hugely important. In fact, you are able to assemble different mixes of your skills to use in a form that is required, in order to display different behavioural roles.

The personal skills we have identified represent a form of inventory of skills that can be mixed and re-assembled to meet a variety of different requirements. This is one of the reasons why people are often surprised to discover they do something well when the pieces are reassembled by chance.

We can use your own personal inventory, produced in the last five chapters, to analyse the nature of successful performance in key areas and to examine the degree of fit between the qualities required and your own personal inventory.

Let's look at the role of a consultant. Whether you are a management consultant or not doesn't really matter. At some time, we are all called in to provide advice and support to others, either internally or to our clients. We all have a mental image of a consultant, yet the role is surprisingly complex and contains a number of very different role models. Here are just a few:

- trouble-shooter
- change agent
- designer
- magician
- coach
- facilitator
- teacher
- specialist
- researcher
- auditor
- analyst

All these roles require different sets of skills and qualities. The type of person who will make a good auditor is quite different from an effective trouble-shooter, which in turn will be quite different from someone who fills a facilitator role.

Review these models and identify which of these roles offer the 'best' and the 'worst' fits to the way you operate at work. Then ask yourself why this is so, by reviewing the personal skills required to fit each role. By the time you have completed this task, you should have gained considerable insight into the critical skills from the overall inventory.

Cultural models

There are very few organisations today that are not international in some sense. The global market is forcing most of us to interact with other cultures on a day-to-day basis. International experience is seen as increasingly important for the new generation of managers entering the world of work. This is reflected in the content of management qualifications, such as the MBA. But it is also reflected in our appreciation of the different cultural perspectives on what makes for successful management.

In fact, many of the models and thinking that percolate into the business community through the latest trend or bestseller on the book lists are themselves strongly culturally biased, in that most of them come from America with a strong Anglo-Saxon influence. Even our understanding of the role of a manager is culturally biased.

For example, examine the four descriptions of a manager below. Which one do you favour and which does your organisation promote?

1 **The traditional view**, based on control, rational analysis and a dislike of uncertainty. Managers are there to steer the organisation through difficulties and to achieve results.
2 **The entrepreneurial view**, based on an experimental approach to life and ability to take on risks. Success is based on creating the future, not waiting for things to happen.
3 **The professional view**, based on technical knowledge and group norms (eg professional). Success is based on the effectiveness of the organisation created through good planning and management.
4 **The humanistic or facilitative approach**, in which the manager seeks to facilitate the work of the group and of individuals. Tasks matter less than the health of the group.

All of these models are legitimate and predominate in different regions of the world and in different organisations. Each has its own advantages and disadvantages. In the last section, we showed you how to build up a range of profiles to match different roles. In just the same way, the personal skills you will need to be successful in any one of these models will be quite different from those required for the other models.

Even in functional areas of management, there are wide differences in approach. In quality management, there is a wide gulf between Total Quality or *kaizen*, based on a more Eastern philosophy, and the hard, Business Process Re-engineering approach.

This point is really important when it comes to your success. One key ingredient in the recipe for success is to make sure that the model that suits you also suits the organisation(s) you work for. This may seem obvious, but creates problems for many managers. Faced with a feeling that things are not going as well as they had liked, there is a natural tendency to say 'maybe I'm not so hot!', but there may be a cultural clash. There are countless examples of people who have known spectacular success or failure simply by changing organisations. Usually the individuals are blamed or praised, but no-one really asks how much the organisational culture is the cause.

Of course, one alternative is to develop the roles and skills associated with different leadership models and, of course, effective managers do indeed do that in developing their emotional intelligence. However, that all takes time and does not cancel out the fact that you are more likely to do well when you work with role models that suit your personality.

Motivation

The fundamental drives that cause us to behave in particular ways are referred to collectively as motivation. In traditional psychology, basic needs and wants drive us towards our goals and orientate us towards particular activities. According to Maslow, there is a hierarchy of needs starting with basic physiological needs, such as food, water and a roof over our head, through social needs right through to our highest ambitions for achievement.

However, this theory is not really very helpful – it certainly doesn't inform us about why we are feeling the way we are, just at this moment. It doesn't explain sudden shifts in emotion and mood or the reasons why people often seek danger or engage in self-destructive activities.

Professor Apter from Georgetown University in America has offered the world a more practical model to explain all this. In his Reversal Theory, he proposes that individuals shift constantly from one mode of thinking to another and that it is often these shifts that bring about our most intense emotions.

His model proposes eight motivational states in four pairs:

Serious, focusing on goals, planning and avoiding surprises or anxiety	**Playful,** focused on enjoyment, acting spontaneously, creating excitement and taking risks
Conforming, orientated towards obligations and the maintenance of rules and routines	**Challenging,** questioning, assumption-testing, orientated towards personal freedom
Mastery, focusing on power, control and dominance	**Sympathy,** driven by security, caring and general harmony
Self-orientated, centred on one's own needs.	**Others-orientated,** in which the needs of others figure most prominently

Each of these states satisfies different emotional needs and we experience them not singly but as combinations of one of each pair, although one or two of these will tend to be more dominant at any point in time. One key argument in the theory is that all eight states contribute to good mental health and that a person needs to become skilful in meeting the needs of all eight states through his/her behaviour and activities. His theory, far from being just a nice piece of academic research, has been able to provide experts with practical tools to improve success in individuals, for example:

- Clinical psychologists and doctors have been able to deal with issues of drug abuse, deviant behaviour and mental illness by using the model to identify the fundamental source of supposedly damaging behaviour.
- Sports coaches have achieved amazing success in athletes by providing them with an emotionally rich environment to work in that deals with issues of boredom and fatigue.
- Organisations are beginning to improve performance by providing a richer emotional environment and checking the correspondence between the supposed culture of the organisation, the key motivating factors for employees and the reality on the 'shop floor'.

So, what does all this mean in practice and how can you use this knowledge to manage your own career more effectively? Well, the main advice we can give is to recognise that the difficulties we experience in exploiting our personal skills to the full come from all this complexity. We need to be realistic and become more aware of our own fluctuations in life, for example:

- Personal action plans are developed as logical and linear plans but they rarely work out that way. Most people go through phases of intense development and progress, followed by periods of relative calm. Look at your personal history – do the peaks come at regular intervals, and are they generally during times of personal upheaval or when conditions are ideal?

- Motivation will go through cycles. Learn to deal with the depression and the disappointments, and learn to turn them into constructive action.
- Ask yourself whether you are getting enough variety in life through your work.

Summary

In this chapter, we have explored some of the more complex factors underlying the application of personal skills and their contribution towards personal success. In particular, we have reviewed the following:

- the relationship between personal skills and the more complex behavioural roles we fulfil
- the role of culture in the fit between you and your organisation
- the importance of motivational factors in success.

In the next chapter, we will review how to make the best of the personal skills inventory that you assessed in Chapters 2 to 5.

Putting it all together

Introduction

So far, we have covered quite a lot. Over the last seven chapters, you should have built up quite a comprehensive profile of your personal skills. In the last chapter, we identified issues that complicated the linkage between this profile and success but that could also offer more insight and control over this repertoire of skills.

In this chapter, we shall provide you with general advice on how to apply this knowledge to further personal development.

Mastering your personal skills inventory

The sheer volume of books on improving personal effectiveness or achieving success, along with the popularity of time management courses and devices to quit smoking, illustrates one key fact – that people generally find it very difficult to change their behaviour. One difficulty people experience in altering behaviour is that it all sounds very easy but in practice is more difficult.

The success factors involved are actually the same as those required to change bad habits, such as smoking or gambling. To change behaviour, you need to remember the following:

- It takes time and patience to achieve significant results.
- You need all the help you can get.
- You have to want to change and this must be linked to clear benefits.

- At the heart of your behaviour lie your basic beliefs and values. Once these change, everything else follows. Unlike practical skills, these values can be changed overnight, but this will only happen through insight or trauma.

You have probably already identified personal skills that you would like to develop. Of course, we can all produce a long list of wishes like 'I wish I were more outgoing, assertive, creative, aware of the needs of others . . .', just like a New Year's resolution list. However, unless we can turn these into action plans, driven by success, the chances are that they will just disappear and be forgotten in time.

To convert self-knowledge of your personal skills into action and success, you need to do three things:

- raise your level of self-awareness, including the source of your motivation
- identify your key development needs and the reasons why you want to change
- create realistic action plans.

Raising your awareness – know thyself

As every good sports coach knows, the key ingredient for improved performance is **raised awareness through constant feedback**. The same principle is used by the masters of martial arts or Zen to achieve almost superhuman feats of strength and skill.

In the workplace, this means we should pay attention to our overall performance on a regular basis (awareness) and overcome any reticence to seek feedback, so that we can improve performance. Frequent and regular feedback is the only way to increase your awareness of your personal skills. Look for different sources – self-assessment tools, your colleagues, your boss, your partner and friends, even customers. Find ways of asking them what they think.

As we discussed in the last chapter, identifying the things that really motivate us to perform well is also important. If we don't have a handle on these and use them to power our development, we are likely to achieve far less in our lives.

Identifying development needs and creating your vision
The self-assessment exercises will certainly have identified things we need to develop. But we also need to link these to the reasons why we seek change. One good place to start is to review your current job, previous career and the effect of your organisation and environment to gain more insight into your personality and what you want from life. For example:

- How well do you suit your current job?
- Which aspects delight you and which do you find frustrating?
- Are you moulding your career to suit your personal preferences and to develop them or is your career changing you?
- How separate is your home and social life from the workplace?
- How different are you outside of work?
- Do you have regrets, things you want to do still?

- If so, why?
- What is your ideal job?
- What is the environment like?
- Who would be your colleagues?
- How would you work and why?

These are dangerous questions to some people, usually because they feel anxious about the answers and don't want to 'take the lid off'. However, they are also liberating questions and critical to keeping your life in your hands. Only by identifying what you want out of life, can you begin to match these aspirations to your personality and identify future action points. Senior managers are particularly prone to ignoring this aspect of their lives; after all, they have reached the top and feel they can't really afford to change direction at this stage.

Creating a realistic action plan designed to ensure success
Assuming that you wish to develop your career, you should use any feedback or self-knowledge to identify priorities for development and an action plan for the future. This is, of course, the difficult part. Here are some general guidelines for developing your action plan.

- **Gauge your readiness for improvement** – just how ready are you to step out into the 'spotlight' and address critical work performance issues?
- **Relate your development needs to your current job and career aspirations** – always check out your feelings and gut reactions to feedback or guidance (such as appraisals) carefully. You may

not want to change. Unless your action plans link up with your core values and personal aspirations, you will find progress difficult.

- **Focus on clear, manageable goals** – build success into your plans. Don't take on too much at once, look for short-term objectives with clear benefits for your career that fit longer-term goals and above all make your objectives SMART – **s**pecific, **m**easurable, **a**chievable, **r**ealistic and **t**ime-constrained.
- **Look for models of best practice** – model your future success on others. Look for people who embody the skills you admire, build in opportunities to watch them at work or even better to work with them, and talk to them about how they think and how they acquired their skills.
- **Set up processes for on-going support and feedback** – as we discussed earlier, your plans need to offer ways of improving self-awareness and feedback, eg:
  - Going it alone is always more difficult. Build your own support network, perhaps with colleagues who meet to discuss common problems. Recruit others to help you practise new skills, such as your boss.
  - Actively seek out feedback on your performance. Don't wait for formal evaluations. Make sure you get positive, constructive feedback. Negative, non-constructive feedback is to be avoided.
  - Learn and master steps for increasing your awareness and self-control.
  - Try to anticipate your 'hot-button' responses to

situations where you do things inappropriately and try to prepare yourself to recognise these and take action. Find a colleague who will signal to you when you are doing something inappropriately.

- **Expect setbacks and build in your own rewards** – if progress seems too hard or slow, consider the possibility that you may be expecting too much from yourself or the organisation. Be more realistic. Allow for setbacks. Success needs reward to sustain it. This simple fact is often overlooked. Find ways of rewarding yourself, even if it is only a special treat. Celebrate your successes.
- **Evaluate progress regularly** – review, review and review! Be realistic and be prepared to adjust your plans if necessary.

General comments on identifying development opportunities

Training programmes are an obvious way of developing your personal skills, but there are many other ways in which you can develop your skills without having to take time away from work or to spend money. In trying to design an action plan for your future development, try to consider a range of in-house solutions that will broaden your practical experience and raise your profile. These might include:

- using a mentor or coach within the organisation to identify development opportunities
- employing a greater variety of assessment tools to

evaluate your skills effectively – ask HR specialists for help in this area
- job shadowing, sharing or exchange schemes; these can be an effective way of learning how others do their work effectively
- special secondments to organisations or units that are centres of excellence for the skills you wish to develop
- participation in company-wide special projects to develop key initiatives
- self-help or action learning groups.

Above all, remember that effective managers possess broad management skills and can operate in a wide variety of situations. Try to avoid just concentrating on development within your professional area of expertise.

And finally . . .

It's a fast-moving world and organisations are becoming very creative about how to get the best out of their people. Keep abreast of these changes by reading round the subject and talking to people from other disciplines. They may be able to point you in the direction of some very simple but effective development tools.

Summary

Creating effective action plans to strengthen personal skills and further success is not always easy. Long-term success will depend on your ability to:

- raise your level of awareness;
- identify your key development needs;
- create realistic action plans and;
- review your plans constantly and keep abreast of the latest developments.

Good luck with your plans.

Resources

Useful addresses

The British Psychological Society (BPS), 48 Princess Road East, Leicester LE1 7DR. Telephone: (0116) 254 9568. Fax: (0116) 247 0787.

The Institute of Management (IM), Management House, Cottingham Road, Corby, Northants, NN17 1TT. Telephone: (01536) 204222.

The Institute of Personnel and Development (IPD), IPD House, Camp Road, London SW19 4UX. Telephone: (020) 8971 9000.

Test suppliers and publishers

Oxford Psychologists Press Ltd, Lambourne House, 311–321 Banbury Road, Oxford, OX2 7JH. Telephone: (01865) 311353.

The Psychological Corporation, Foots Cray, High Street, Sidcup DA14 5HP.

Psytech International Ltd, The Grange, Church Road, Pulloxhill, Beds, MK45 5HE. Telephone: (01525) 720003.

Saville & Holdsworth Ltd, 3 AC Court, High Street, Thames Ditton, Surrey, KT7 0SR. Telephone. (020) 8398 4170.

The Test Agency, Cray House, Woodlands Road, Henley on Thames, Oxon, RG9 4AE. Telephone: (01491) 413413.

Further reading

Boyatzis, R, *The Competent Manager: A model for effective performance*, John Wiley & Sons (1982).

Crozier, G, *Test Your Personality*, Hodder & Stoughton (2000).

Goleman, D, *Emotional Intelligence*, Bantam Books (1995).

O'Neill, B, *Test Your Leadership Skills*, Hodder & Stoughton (2000).

Pearn, M & Kandola, R, *Job Analysis: A practical guide for managers*, IPM (1988).

Senge, P M, Kleiner, A, Roberts, C, Ross, R & Smith, B, *The Fifth Discipline Fieldbook*, Nicholas Brealey Publishing Ltd (1994).

Smith, M & Robertson, I, *Advances in Selection and Assessment*, John Wiley & Sons (1993).